GECKOS AND
THEIR RELATIVES...

ERIK D. STOOPS

Faulkner's Publishing Group

This book is dedicated to Wai Lui, for his outstanding contribution to and knowledge of these wonderful reptiles, and Lori Stelmacher for her help in making these books happen.

Library of Congress Catalog Card Number 97-60520.

COVER PHOTO: Leopard Gecko by Terry Odegaard
DESIGNED BY: Graphic Arts & Production, Inc., Plover, WI

Faulkner's Publishing Group
200 Paw Paw Ave. #124
Benton Harbor, MI 49022

©1997 by Erik Daniel Stoops
Faulkner's ISBN 1-890475-00-9 Lib

Table of Contents

5/99 Gumdrop 12 83

Chapter One

What are Geckos and their Relatives?

What is a Gecko?

What do lizards die from?

Read on to discover these answers and more.

What is a Gecko?

A Gecko is a reptile. These reptiles have four legs for walking and climbing. They usually have a large powerful tail, eyelids and ears. Some lizards do not have legs at all. **Scientists** have found that certain lizard species are related to their cousin, the snake. Scientists have found that Geckos first appeared on the earth fifty million years ago.

LEOPARD GECKOS ARE POPULAR IN THE PET TRADE. THEY MAKE WONDERFUL ANIMALS TO KEEP IN A TERRARIUM.
▼

Are lizards cold-blooded or warm-blooded?

All species of lizards are **cold-blooded**. They need the warm sun during the day to help them move and digest their food.

What do lizards die from?

Many lizards die from diseases such as cancer, heart disease and tumors because they don't get enough exercise when held in captivity. Lizards can catch colds and cough and sneeze like we do. They also can die from **parasites** that crawl on their body. **Poachers** may often kill lizards for their skin or catch lizards to sell to people. This is not very fair to the lizards.

by Terry Odegaard

5

If I want to see a Gecko, where should I look?

The safest place to see a Gecko is at the zoo. Many zoos have several kinds of species on display from all over the world. It is best not to catch lizards from the wild and keep them in your home. Try to leave them where they belong.

THE LEOPARD GECKO IS ONE SPECIES OF LIZARD YOU COULD SEE AT YOUR LOCAL ZOO.
▼

by Terry Odegaard

6

What is the difference between a Salamander and a Gecko?

A Gecko and a Salamander are similar because they both are cold-blooded. However, a Salamander is classified as an amphibian because it is scaleless and lives in water and land. Whereas the Gecko is a reptile that has scales and lives in trees.

THE TIGER SALAMANDER ▶
LOOKS LIKE A LARGE
GECKO BUT HAS MANY
DIFFERENT HABITS AS
AN AMPHIBIAN.

by Terry Odegaard

THE NEWT IS NOT A
GECKO EITHER, BUT IS A ▶
KIND OF SALAMANDER.

by Terry Odegaard

7

Do lizards have suction cups on their feet?

Geckos have special toe-pads which give them the ability to walk up and down smooth walls and ceilings. Some species can do this so well that it helps them catch food. According to scientists, each toe-pad consists of 100 to 1000 extremely small suction cups. If you looked under an electronic microscope, these would be clearly visible. This is what makes Geckos awesome acrobats of the lizard world.

Can Geckos climb trees?

Yes. Geckos of the rain forest spend much of their lives in trees and are found to be wonderful climbers. They can also be found in people's houses in South America where they help keep the insect population down.

by Pat Turcott

◀ THE TOE-PADS OF THE MADAGASCAR DAY GECKO HELPS IT CLIMB UP SMOOTH SURFACES SUCH AS GLASS AND WALLS. THESE TWO MADAGASCAR DAY GECKOS ARE RESTING ON A GLASS WINDOW.

by Pat Turcott

8

GECKOS

Tokay Gecko:

This large Gecko is found throughout Southeast Asia. They are a gray color, spotted with orange and red dots. They make a strange noise during the mating season which sounds like "To-Keh" or "Geck-Oh." They feed on insects and small lizards. They can grow up to 12 inches in length.

Banded Gecko:

The Banded Gecko is found in dry regions of western North America. Unlike most Gecko species they lack toe-pads and are one of the few Geckos that have functional eyelids. When catching food, crickets for example, they hunt like a cat, pouncing on its victim. They lay 2-3 eggs in midsummer. An adult can reach the length of 4 inches.

THE TOKAY GECKO ▶ IS ONE OF THE LARGEST SPECIES OF GECKOS FOUND IN THE WORLD.

by Scottsdale Children's Nature Center

9

Chapter Two

Where are Geckos and their Relatives Found?

Where is the best place to find a Gecko?

What type of habitat does a Gecko like?

Read on to discover these answers and more.

Where are Geckos found?

Geckos are found all over the world except Antarctica. Many species are found in rain forests. They spend a lot of their time in trees and bushes.

THIS LEOPARD GECKO IS AT HOME ▶ ON HIS ROCK.

by Terry Odegaard

by Wai Lui

▲ THE ASIAN DESERT GECKO LIKES HOT WEATHER.

What type of habitat does a Gecko like?

Some species like the Banded Gecko, live in the desert of southwestern United States. Other species, such as the Madagascar Leaf-Tailed Gecko, live in thick rain forests.

Where is the best place to find a Gecko?

If I were a Gecko, this is where I would be:

- Under a rock
- On a rock
- In a field
- On a house
- In a tree
- In a rain forest

by Terry Odegaard

▲ MANY SPECIES OF LIZARDS MAKE THEIR HOMES IN LARGE TREES LIKE THIS ONE.

Chapter Three

Senses

Do Geckos make noises?

How do Geckos use their tongues?

This chapter will answer some of the important questions about lizards' senses.

Can lizards make noises?

Yes. The only species of lizards that have vocalization are Geckos. When frightened, they chirp or screech which sounds like a cat's meow. These are the only species of lizards that can do this. Scientists have found that these cries, if you listen carefully, sound like the word "geck-o."

by Terry Odegaard

Do Geckos have tongues and what are they used for?

Geckos use their tongue for many different things. They use them to smell, taste, to feel the vibrations in the air and on the ground, as well as to eat with. They also use their tongue to drink with.

Do Geckos have good eyesight?

Yes. Geckos have outstanding eyesight. The House Gecko can see a meal such as a fly or a cricket from several yards away. Almost all species of Geckos are nocturnal. This means they come out at night.

WHEN THE LEAF-TAILED GECKO IS SCARED IT WILL OFTEN MAKE CHIRPING NOISES.
▼

13

Do lizards have noses?

Yes. The snout of a lizard is located on its head. It has two nostrils which it uses to breathe with.

Do lizards use their tongues only to smell?

No. Some lizards use their noses to smell also. The Jacobson's organ helps lizards smell through their tongues. This is a small organ located behind the lizard's tongue.

Do lizards have feelings?

According to scientists, lizards can feel pain. All animal species can feel pain. When an animal is hurt, their wounds heal the same as our wounds do.

Do Geckos have eyelids?

All lizards have eyelids. This is what makes them different from their cousin, the snake. Although all Geckos have eyelids, some species' eyelids are non-functional such as the Banded Gecko.

SAND GECKO
▼

by Wai Lu

14

What does albino mean?

The word albino means loss of normal coloration or pigment in the skin. Animals that are born albino in the wild usually do not live very long because they cannot blend in with their surroundings.

by Wai Lui

▲

AS YOU CAN SEE, THIS ALBINO AUSTRALIAN VELVET GECKO HAS VERY LITTLE COLORATION.

ENT TOE GECKO

Are there any albino Geckos?

According to scientists, there have been many albinos found throughout the world, such as the Albino Gecko in this photo.

by Wai Lui

15

Chapter Four

Eating Habits

What do Geckos eat?

How do Geckos capture their prey?

Read on and try to find the answers.

How do Geckos capture their prey?

They wait for their prey to come into view and then pounce on it like a cat, swallowing it quickly. Lizards use their eyesight and their strong sense of smell to find their food. Insect-eating lizards may stay at a cricket nest and feed until all are full.

How often do Geckos eat?

Some species eat every day like the Banded Gecko, while the Tokay Gecko might eat three times a week. Geckos can eat a large meal such as many crickets or insects and store food in their tail.

What do Geckos eat?

All species of Geckos are carnivores (car-na-vores). They enjoy feeding on insects such as ants, flies, crickets and spiders.

THIS LEOPARD GECKO ▶ HAS A LARGE BULKY TAIL. GECKOS WILL STORE FOOD IN THEIR TAIL DURING CERTAIN TIMES OF THE YEAR. FOR EXAMPLE, DURING WEATHER CHANGES OR HIBERNATION.

by Terry Odegaard

17

Do Geckos have taste buds?

Yes. According to scientists, Geckos can taste their food. This is how they determine what type of food they will eat.

Do Geckos have enemies?

Yes. Birds, rats and even house cats catch Geckos and eat them. Most Geckos hide during the day and are active at night to avoid these enemies.

by Wai Lui

THIS WEB-FOOTED GECKO WILL OFTEN DIG A HOLE AND WAIT IN IT FOR ITS PREY TO WALK BY, THEN POUNCE ON IT LIKE A CAT.

Do Geckos have sharp teeth used to chew their food?

No. Lizards do not chew their food. They swallow it whole after gulping it.

Do Geckos eat other lizards?

Yes. The Tokay Gecko has a very powerful jaw which allows it to feed on mice, small birds and any young lizards.

by Wai Lui

THIS AUSTRALIAN VELVET GECKO
IS HIDING FROM ITS ENEMIES ON A LOG.

19

Chapter Five

Lizard Reproduction

How do Geckos lay eggs?

How can you tell the difference between the male and female?

Read on and try to find the answers.

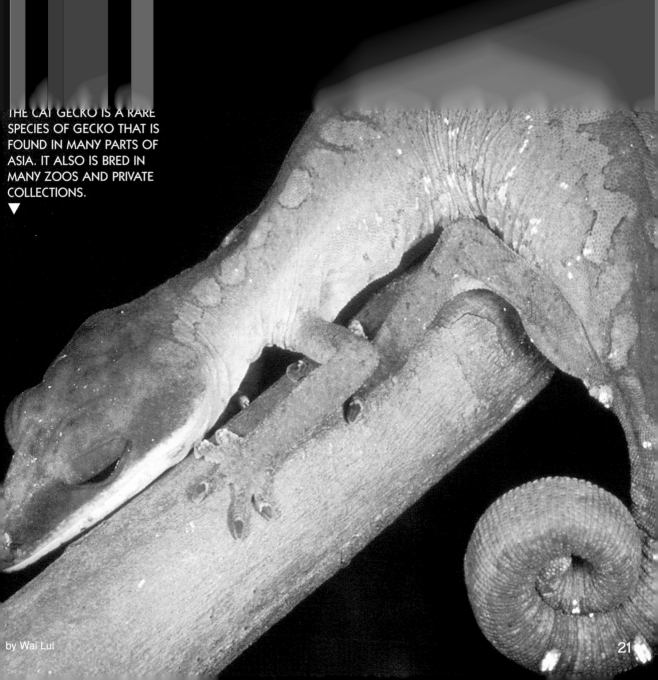

THE CAT GECKO IS A RARE SPECIES OF GECKO THAT IS FOUND IN MANY PARTS OF ASIA. IT ALSO IS BRED IN MANY ZOOS AND PRIVATE COLLECTIONS.

▼

by Wai Lui

When do Geckos mate?

When Geckos mate depends on the species and where it is found during the spring or the rainy season. In parts of the United States, Geckos mate after hibernation.

How can you tell the difference between the male and female?

In some species of Geckos, males may be more colorful or larger than the female. In other species such as Tokay Geckos, males may have larger tails than females. Male lizards have hemi-penes located in the anal plate which is used for mating.

by Terry Odegaard

AFTER GECKOS HATCH FROM THEIR EGGS, THEY START LOOKING FOR FOOD.

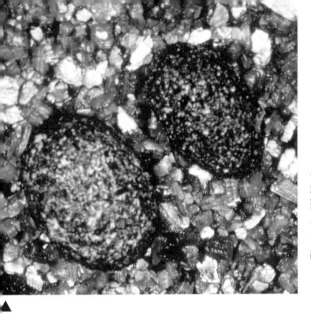

Photos by Wai Lui

▲
HESE CAT GECKO EGGS ARE VERY SMALL.

▲
HATCHING CAT GECKO EGGS.

How can you tell if a lizard is pregnant?

After mating, females will how signs of pregnancy in a couple of different ways. The House Gecko may have ncreased swelling near the tomach area, and you can actually see the eggs inside he belly area. At this time, many Gecko species will eed or eat twice as much.

Do Geckos lay hard or soft eggs?

Geckos lay soft eggs which turn hard after a few hours. Some species such as Day Geckos lay eggs that stick together. The House Gecko will often lay eggs on the side of a wall or in the cracks in a wall.

How do Geckos lay eggs?

As an egg-laying species, the House Gecko will often bury her eggs for 6-8 weeks in a safe, warm, moist place. Female Geckos lay eggs through their *anal plate,* which is located at the base of the tail between the hind legs. She will never see her babies again.

23

Chapter Six

Self-Defense

How does a Gecko protect itself?

Do Geckos bite?

Read on to discover these answers and more.

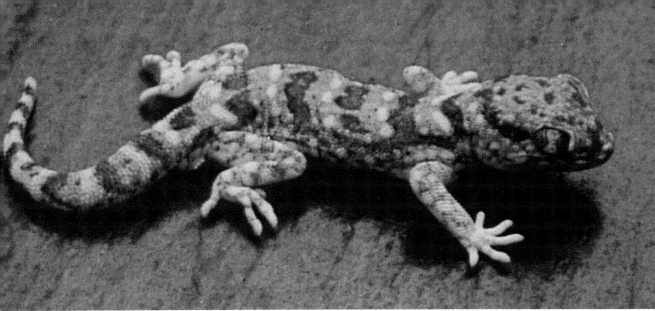

by Wai Lui

▲
THIS RARE SAND GECKO IS ABLE TO
HIDE FROM ITS ENEMIES IN THE SAND.

How do Geckos protect themselves?

Some species of Geckos make large chirping sounds when alarmed, while others can actually play dead. When the enemies go away the Gecko runs and hides.

What about their colors?

This is the best self-defense a Gecko has. The Madagascar Leaf-Tailed Gecko can blend into its surroundings so well that you can look at a tree with one on it and never even see it.

Can a Gecko bite?

Most are too small to bite but the Tokay Gecko can give a person a nasty bite. You should never make a Gecko bite you. This does more harm to the lizard than to you. If you see a Gecko, you should just leave it alone.

Chapter Seven

Facts about Geckos and their Relatives

What are the largest and smallest species of Geckos?

Can Geckos jump out of their skin?

Read on to discover these answers and more.

et's classify a Gecko:

he *family* of Gecko is Gekkonidae.

species of Gekkonidae
a Tokay Gecko.

e pronounce the
amily name
Gekk-on-in-dee).
ow you give it a try.

How many species of Geckos are there?

According to scientists there are about 800 species found throughout the world.

by Wai Lu

FRICAN FAT-TAILED GECKO

▲
THIS LUII GECKO IS VERY RARE.

by Wai Lui

27

What do Geckos use their tail for?

Some species of Geckos store food or fat in their tail. The New Zealand Green Tree Gecko actually uses its tail to hang from such things as tree branches.

Can Geckos jump out of their skin?

Some species of Geckos, when frightened, can actually jump out of their skin. This is usually only in extreme cases and the Gecko will die after this tragic self-defense.

▲ NEW CALEDONIA CRESTED GECKO

by Wai Lui

◀ THIS NEW ▶
SPECIES
OF GECKO
IS CALLED
THE LUII
GECKO.

by Wai Lui

What is the largest Gecko?

The New Caledonia Geckos are the largest species of geckos in the world. They can reach a length of 16 inches.

What are the smallest species of Geckos?

According to scientists, the Geckos of the Genus Saurodactylus are the smallest species of lizards. An adult is about 3 inches in length. They are rare and not often seen in the wild. They are found in Morocco, Algeria in Africa.

Glossary

Anal Plate:
The large scale between the back legs of the lizard.

Chlamydosaurus King II:
A scientific name for frilled lizard.

Cold-Blooded:
Having a body temperature not internally regulated, but approximately that of the environment.

Endangered: Threatened with extinction.

Endemic:
Native to a particular country, nation or region.

External:
Having merely the outward appearance of something.

Fossil:
A remnant impression, or trace of an animal or plant of past geological ages that has been preserved in the earth's crust.

Herpetologist:
One who studies reptiles and amphibians.

Neonate: Newborn.

Paleontologist:
One who studies the science dealing with the life of past geological periods as known from fossil remains.

Parasite:
An organism that lives in or on another organism at whose expense it receives nourishment.

Poacher:
One who kills or takes game and fish illegally.

Quadrupole:
A system composed of two dipoles of equal but oppositely directed moment.

Rhynchocephalian:
A class of reptile.

Scientist:
A scientific investigator.

Unisexual:
All individuals are females that can lay eggs and are fertile without mating.

Virus:
The causative agent of an infectious disease.

Warm-Blooded:
Having a relatively high and constant body temperature relatively independent of the surroundings.

Books and CD-Roms Written by the Author Suggested Reading

Snakes and Other Reptiles of the Southwest

Erik D. Stoops & Annette T. Wright. 1991. Golden West Publishing Company, Phoenix, Arizona. Scientific Field Guide.

Snakes

Erik D. Stoops & Annette T. Wright. 1992. Hardback and Paperback. Sterling Publishing Company, New York. Children's non-fiction, full-color, question and answer format. First Book in Children's Nature Library Series.

Breeding Boas and Pythons

Erik D. Stoops & Annette T. Wright. 1993. TFH Publishing Company, New York. Scientific Care and Breeding Guide.

Sharks

Erik D. Stoops & Sherrie L. Stoops. Illustrated by Jeffrey L. Martin. June, 1994. Hardback and Paperback. Sterling Publishing Company, New York. Children's non-fiction, full-color, question and answer format. Second Book in Children's Nature Library Series.

Dolphins

Erik D. Stoops, Jeffrey L. Martin & Debbie L. Stone. Release date, January, 1995. Hardback and Paperback. Sterling Publishing Company, New York. Children's non-fiction, full-color, question and answer format. Third Book in Children's Nature Library Series.

Whales

Erik D. Stoops, Jeffrey L. Martin & Debbie L. Stone. Release date, March, 1995. Hardback and Paperback. Sterling Publishing Company, New York. Children's non-fiction, full-color, question and answer format. Fourth Book in Children's Nature Library Series.

Scorpions and Other Venomous Insects of the Desert

Erik D. Stoops & Jeffrey L. Martin. Release date, June, 1995. Golden West Publishing Company, Phoenix, Arizona. A user-friendly guide.

Alligators and Crocodiles

Erik D. Stoops & Debbie L. Stone. Release date, October, 1994. Sterling Publishing Company, New York. Children's non-fiction, full-color, question and answer format. Fifth Book in Children's Nature Library Series.

Wolves

Erik D. Stoops & Dagmar Fertl. Release date, December, 1996. Sterling Publishing Company, New York. Children's non-fiction, full-color, question and answer format. Sixth Book in Children's Nature Library Series.

Internet Sites:

Zoo Net:
http://www.mindspring.com/~zoonet

Herp Link:
http://home.ptd.net/~herplink/index.html

Erik Stoops:
http://www.primenet.com/~dink

Look for the Adventures of Dink the Skink Children's book series and animated CD Rom Stories coming out in 1997.

INDEX

WE WOULD LIKE TO THANK THE FOLLOWING PEOPLE FOR THEIR ENCOURAGEMENT AND PARTICIPATION:
NATIONAL ZOOLOGICAL PARK, OFFICE OF PUBLIC AFFAIRS, SUSAN BIGGS, SMITHSONIAN INSTITUTION,
TERRY CHRISTOPHER, TERRY ODEGAARD, CINCINNATI ZOO AND BOTANICAL GARDENS, ST. LOUIS ZOO,
BILL LUBACK'S REPTILES, INC., AMANDA JAKSHA, JESSIE COHEN, PAT TURCOTT, RODNEY FREEMAN,
DIANE E. FREEMAN, STEVEN CASTANEDA, CLYDE PEELINGS OF REPTILELAND, MICKEY OLSEN OF WILDLIFE
WORLD ZOO, SCOTTSDALE CHILDREN'S NATURE CENTER, DR. JEAN ARNOLD, ARIZONA GAME AND
FISH DEPARTMENT, ERIN DEAN OF THE UNITED STATES FISH AND WILDLIFE SERVICE,
BOB FAULKNER, DAVE PFEIFFER OF EDUCATION ON WHEELS FOR MAKING THIS PROJECT A REALITY,
DR. MARTY FELDMAN, SHERRIE STOOPS, ALESHA STOOPS, VICTORIA AND JESSICA EMERY.